The Baran Method

Writing for Success

Greg Baran

Copyright © 2019 by Greg Baran. All rights reserved.
No part of this publication may be reproduced, distributed, or transmitted in any form or any means, including, but not limited to, photocopying, recording, or other electronic or mechanical methods, without the prior written permission of the author, except in the case of brief quotations in critical reviews and certain other noncommercial uses permitted by copyright laws. For permissions, e-mail the author at greg@gregbaranwriting.com.

To my wife, Heather.
Far too many times this work, this method,
and this book have taken me from your side—but
you were never far from my heart. I am eternally
grateful for you. I could not have completed any
of this work without your love, patience, and support.
Thank You! Thank You! Thank You!

Contents

Free *Baran Method* Resources

Reviews of *The Baran Method*

Preface

Introduction

Instructions

    CEA Paragraph

    CEA Essay

Final Thoughts

CEA Paragraph Map

Claim Poster

Supporting Detail Poster

Evidence Poster

Analysis of Evidence Poster

Summation Poster

Thesis Poster

CEA Paragraph Checklist Poster

CEA Paragraph Checklist with Comments

CEA Paragraph Self/Peer Review Worksheet

Transitions

CEA Traditional Essay Map

CEA Traditional Essay Checklist

CEA Non-Traditional Essay Map

CEA Non-Traditional Essay Checklist

Example Paragraph and Essay Instructions

Example Paragraphs and Essays

Free *Baran Method* Resources

gregbaranwriting.com/resources

To help guide your through this easy process, I created a free web resource at gregbaranwriting.com/resources with grade-specific paragraph and essay examples. I highly recommend you sign up now. These models are organized by grade levels, making it easier to find and work with the material as you quickly learn the Baran Method. Over time, I'll be adding material, so make sure to sign up now and get free access to the content!

Feel free to contact me if you have any questions or want personal coaching or group workshops at greg@gregbaranwriting.com or Ph. (760) 459-5597.

Reviews of *The Baran Method*

"As a new teacher, I struggled with teaching writing, especially essays. This method helped make the teaching process much less frustrating for me and the learning process much less frustrating for my students. That's a win-win in my book! I'm glad I found this."
— Alex B.

"I bought this book for my high school granddaughter thinking she could use the method to improve her skills in preparation for college and business applications. It has helped her better organize her thoughts and school notes and made assigned writing easier, more enjoyable for her, and more interesting to read when finished."
— Barbara M.

"Having read this book, I can honestly say my writing has really improved. This book explains the structure of essays and explains it in great detail. Not only is it filled with specific directions on how to properly write essays, it has color-coordinated maps that show how to write essays. This method can really help anyone who is struggling to learn how to write. The book is not lengthy, yet filled with great information. I highly recommend it to anyone who needs help with any writing assignment!"
— Esteban O.

Preface

All children have wonderful ideas. *In order to be successful, our children need to be able to write these ideas clearly—and as parents, we need to be able to assure ourselves our children are being given the best opportunity to succeed.*

At this time in our history, the need to write and communicate effectively is paramount in our personal and business lives. Today, most of our written communications are electronic, especially in the professional world. This speed of communication magnifies the need to communicate clearly. The foundation for opportunity and success in the professional world begins at the elementary level and continues throughout the educational process. Well-written paragraphs and essays created early in our lives form the foundation for the reports we write later that directly affect our upward mobility in the professional world. Consequently, being able to write effectively and clearly is the key to our children's success.

For children and adults gaining this ability is both possible and simple—and everyone can learn to how to do so. It's not complicated. We just need a *clear* understanding of the structures of *clear* communication. This method will give everyone willing to use it a very clear understanding. It doesn't take long and it is not arduous.

I'm glad you're here. Thanks for allowing me to join you on this journey.

Happy Writing!
Greg Baran

The Baran Method
Writing for Success

Introduction

Claim, evidence, and analysis (CEA)—these are the fundamental and foundational concepts for any successful exposition or argument. Every effective paragraph or essay needs a claim, or statement of purpose, followed by evidence to support the claim, and then analysis that shows how the evidence proves the claim. For writers to become more effective, mastering the use of these rhetorical concepts is paramount? This handbook sets writers on the road to mastery by specifically mapping out the rhetorical function and "locations" for claim, evidence, and analysis in successful academic writing, but the concepts work for non-academic writing as well. Additionally, this guide will help instructors from any discipline and/or homeschool setting become confident writing teachers.

The maps are the heart of this guide. *Because the purpose and placement for each sentence is shown in the maps, writers can focus on what to say and not worry about where to say it.* Indeed, by showing the specific task for each sentence in the paragraph or essay, the maps make paragraph and essay writing more accessible and understandable to writers at any grade level or ability—from elementary school through college—or beyond. This approach is not a formula, but a structured framework. The framework helps writers organize their thoughts in a concise and easy-to-understand manner. Once writers comprehend the basic paragraph and essay structure, then they are ready for more complex writing. The end goal is for writers to learn the rhetorical basics of writing and then move on to more elaborate and in-depth writing and analysis without the need for a map of any kind.

In essence then, the main purpose for this handbook is to take the mystery out of formal writing and to give every writer specific tools to become more effective. The following instructions, maps, and resources will guide teachers and writers at all levels through the writing process and example paragraphs and essays at the end of the handbook will serve as models.

Instructions

CEA Paragraph Map

The first map is the paragraph map. This map shows the purpose for each sentence in the paragraph and provides a direct guide for crafting a single paragraph. Each sentence in the map is color coded and utilizes a corresponding symbol to make comprehension easier. For teachers, and all writers, this key visual works best when referred to consistently for everyday writing, homework, or other paragraph building activities. Gluing in or attaching the document to a notebook effectively keeps the document close at hand. In addition, the map can be turned into a poster, placed on a wall, and referred to throughout instruction.

Each line of the map represents one sentence of the paragraph. There are five sentences in the paragraph: claim, supporting detail, evidence, analysis of evidence, and summation. Each sentence serves a specific purpose or "job." Together, these five sentences create a rhetorically sound paragraph. In other words, when used together these components create an effective and solid argument or exposition. This approach helps writers "see" and comprehend the basic symmetry and structure of a formal or academic paragraph. At times, altering this structure is a necessity, but in the beginning following this general order results in faster comprehension.

The first sentence of the paragraph map is the claim or paragraph topic, which is also sometimes called the central or main idea. In this sentence, the writer tells the reader the topic of the paragraph, which is why the megaphone symbol is used. Next, a supporting detail is written, such as a definition of a term in the claim or expansion on the claim. The symbol of a stool reminds the writer their claim needs support, especially when further information is needed to explain the claim or help the reader better understand the claim. The next sentence is the evidence (quote, statistic, interview, paraphrase, etc.) that proves the writer's claim. This sentence usually begins with "According to [name of author] … " or "[Name of author] states/writes." A magnifying glass reminds writers they need to offer a strong piece of evidence—quote, facts, or other information—that validates the claim.

The following sentence, analysis of evidence, examines how or why the evidence proves the claim. This sentence usually begins with, "This quote shows/demonstrates …" or "This passage reveals … " or a similar transition. The microscope symbolizes that this is the time to examine and study the evidence for meaning. The ultimate goal is to show how the evidence proves the claim. The last sentence of the paragraph, summation, serves as further analysis while its major intent is to sum up the paragraph. This sentence generally begins with a *showing a result* transition word(s) like, "Consequently, ..." or "Therefore, ..." or "As a result, ... ". A gift box symbolizes wrapping up the analysis and information provided (in an essay, this sentence would also connect the paragraph back to the thesis).

Following the paragraph map are the posters with corresponding symbols that further explain each paragraph sentence and concept. Additionally, there is a thesis poster for essay writing that explains the purpose of a thesis. These posters will guide the writer as they work with each concept. In a classroom setting, the posters can be posted, given directly to the writer, and/or projected.

Finally, a CEA paragraph checklist and self/peer paragraph review worksheet follows the posters and allows writers to self-assess and/or evaluate each other. A list of commonly used transitions is also included.

CEA Essay Maps

Like the paragraph map, the two essay maps have several uses including explanatory/expository, argumentative/persuasive, literary analysis, critical analysis, compare and contrast, descriptive, and summative essays. Also similar to the paragraph map, the essay maps are meant to be referred to repeatedly during the writing process. In regard to the structure of the essay maps, the maps use the traditional and logical 5-paragraph structure. Line spacing is 1.5, but this is only so the map fits on one page and is thus easier to follow. When writing, it is recommended that writers follow the traditional collegial format of double spacing, 12 point font, and a legible font choice.

Like the paragraph map, each line of the essay map represents one sentence in the essay. Each essay map has five paragraphs: an introduction, three body paragraphs, and a conclusion. As writers work to master the CEA paragraph, they are also working toward mastering the 5-paragraph essay since the essay body paragraphs are the same format as the single CEA paragraph. In fact, one way—and sometimes a quicker way—to learn how to write an essay is to write the body paragraphs first *and then* write the introduction and conclusion.

Before we can move on, a side note must be added in regard to thesis and claim before further explanation of the essay maps. The thesis can rightly be described as the overarching claim, or central idea, of the entire essay. Indeed, in a classroom it is helpful to remind writers the thesis and overarching claim are synonymous, yet they need to know each paragraph will have its own claim, or topic sentence, as well. This concept may be confusing and should be addressed. Finally, the thesis in the essay maps is not marked in blue like the paragraph claims. Instead, the thesis is highlighted in yellow to signify its role as the main idea of the entire essay.

The first essay map is *traditional* with a "hook" to open the introduction and the thesis at the end of the introduction. After the hook, the second sentence introduces the essay topic. Next, the claim for Body Paragraph 1 is stated. This is followed by the claim for Body Paragraph 2. Finally, the claim for Body Paragraph 3 is stated. The introduction ends in the traditional manner with the thesis as the last sentence of the introduction.

The second map is *non-traditional* with the thesis as the first sentence of the introduction. For many writers, the *non-traditional* approach is recommended since they do not need to craft a creative hook and can "jump" right into the essay. As a result, many writers find the writing process becomes more linear and thus easier to grasp. After the thesis, the next three sentences introduce the claims for Body Paragraphs 1, 2, and 3. The introduction concludes with a transition sentence that shifts the focus to the body of the essay.

For both maps, once the introduction is complete students should literally follow the arrows that show the paragraph claim for each body paragraph being transferred "down" (or copied and pasted) to its corresponding body paragraph position and rephrased. In this context, "rephrase" does not mean rework the entire sentence. Altering (finding synonyms for) or "flip-flopping" clauses is enough for writers to demonstrate rhetorical understanding while avoiding simply copying and pasting. The example essays at the end of the handbook will serve to illustrate this concept.

Also for both essay maps, Body Paragraph 1 begins with the claim from the introduction being restated and rephrased. The rest of Body Paragraph 1 follows the same pattern as the CEA paragraph map: claim, supporting detail, evidence, analysis of evidence, and summation (in an essay, this sentence connects the paragraph back to the thesis). Body Paragraphs 2 and 3 follow the same structure.

The conclusion for the *traditional* and *non-traditional* maps are the same, with one exception. For the *traditional* map , the conclusion begins with a standard transition.

However, when using the *non-traditional* map, the conclusion begins by simply restating and rephrasing the last sentence of the introduction. With either map, after the first sentence of the conclusion writers will restate and rephrase the thesis. Then, Body Paragraphs 1, 2, and 3 are synthesized and blended into one sentence. The last sentence of the essay is generally a creative summation of the piece leaving the reader with a feeling they learned something from the writer. Finally, after each map a checklist follows for self/peer review assessment purposes.

In conclusion, many developing writers will notice the repetition in the map structure. The response to this valid observation is that that their observation is absolutely correct. It is beneficial for writers to understand that any effective essay circles back to the thesis and body paragraph claims regularly, using synonyms to modify and alter the repetitive "flow," but not the essay's meaning. In the end, the goal is for writers to comprehend the fundamentals of paragraph and essay structure, and repetition is definitely a major component.

Final Thoughts

Last but certainly not least, make sure to frequently refer to the exemplar paragraphs and essays in the last section of the handbook. Along with using the maps, seeing effective writing is key to quickly mastering writing. Indeed, you'll find these models really help speed up the learning process since they show what an effective final product should look like—and remember, there are additional grade-specific paragraph and essay examples at gregbaranwriting.com/resources.

All the best. Happy Writing!
Greg Baran

P.S. Feel free to contact me if you have any questions or want personal coaching or group workshops at greg@gregbaranwriting.com or Ph. (760) 459-5597.

Maps and Posters

CEA

Claim - Evidence - Analysis

Write an effective paragraph in 5 sentences

Claim for Paragraph
- What point are you trying to make?
- What do you want the reader to understand about the issue?

Supporting Detail for Claim
- Provide information about the topic of your paragraph.
- Support might define an unfamiliar term or help further explain your topic.

Evidence from Text
- Use a phrase, sentence, or facts from the text to provide evidence for your claim.
- Introduce the evidence like this: According to [the author's name], "..." or [the author's name] states, "..."

Analysis of Evidence
- What does your evidence mean?
- How does your evidence prove your claim?
- Use sentence starters like: This quote shows... or This passage reveals... or The author is stating that...

Summation
- Finish the paragraph by summing and wrapping up your ideas.
- Show inferences by using transition words like: Therefore, ... or Consequently, ... or As a result, ... or For this reason, ...

Claim for Paragraph

- **This is the topic or main idea of the paragraph.**
- **The claim explains the paragraph's purpose.**
- **What point are you trying to make?**
- **What do you want the reader to understand about the issue?**
- **In an essay, stay focused on the paragraph's claim and how it connects to the essay's thesis.**

Supporting Detail for Claim

- Provides information about the claim/topic of your paragraph.
- Support helps you further explain your topic.
- Support helps your reader further understand your topic.
- Support might define an unfamiliar term.
- Support might define a concept or idea.

Evidence from Text

- Use a phrase, sentence, passage, or interview from the text to provide evidence for your claim.
- Evidence can also include facts, statistics, reasons, or an example.
- Evidence makes your claim legitimate.
- Introduce the evidence like this: According to [the author's name], "…" or [the author's name] states, "…"

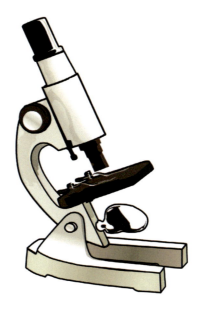

Analysis of Evidence

- Shows how your evidence proves your claim.
- Tells the reader what your evidence means.
- Explains the significance of your evidence.
- Shows why the evidence is important to your paragraph claim and thesis.
- Use sentence starters like: This quote shows… or This passage reveals… or The author is stating that…

Summation

- **Finish the paragraph by summing and wrapping up your ideas.**
- **Reassert how your evidence is important to your claim.**
- **Connect the evidence and claim to your thesis.**
- **Show inferences by using transition words like: Therefore, … or Consequently, … or As a result, . . . or For this reason, …**

Thesis

- The main idea, message, or key point/s in an essay.

- Expresses and summarizes the essay's purpose.

- Acts as a guide to the ideas, opinions, facts, and analysis you will discuss in the essay.

- Organizes and presents the order ideas, facts, and analysis will appear in the essay.

- Usually located in the first/introductory paragraph of an essay.

CEA Paragraph Checklist

- ☐ **Claim**

- ☐ **Supporting Detail**

- ☐ **Evidence**

- ☐ **Analysis of Evidence**

- ☐ **Summation**

CEA Paragraph Checklist

- ❏ **Claim**　　　　　　　　　Comment _____
- ❏ **Supporting Detail**　　　Comment _____
- ❏ **Evidence**　　　　　　　Comment _____
- ❏ **Analysis of Evidence**　Comment _____
- ❏ **Summation**　　　　　　Comment _____

CEA Paragraph Checklist

- ❏ **Claim**　　　　　　　　　Comment _____
- ❏ **Supporting Detail**　　　Comment _____
- ❏ **Evidence**　　　　　　　Comment _____
- ❏ **Analysis of Evidence**　Comment _____
- ❏ **Summation**　　　　　　Comment _____

Writing a CEA Paragraph — **Self Review**

Name _____

- Paragraph starts with a topic sentence and includes a claim _____ / 3
- Supporting detail for the claim is included _____ / 3
- Evidence from the text is included _____ / 3
- Evidence proves/supports the claim _____ / 3
- Evidence is cited _____ / 3
- Evidence is analyzed for meaning _____ / 3
- Paragraph is summed up _____ / 3
- Appropriate transition words are included _____ / 3
- Sentences are clear and make sense _____ / 3
- Spelling and punctuation are accurate _____ / 3

Total _____ / 30

Writing a CEA Paragraph — **Peer Review**

Name _____

Peer Reviewer Name _____

- Paragraph starts with a topic sentence and includes a claim _____ / 3
- Supporting detail for the claim is included _____ / 3
- Evidence from the text is included _____ / 3
- Evidence proves/supports the claim _____ / 3
- Evidence is cited _____ / 3
- Evidence is analyzed for meaning _____ / 3
- Paragraph is summed up _____ / 3
- Appropriate transition words are included _____ / 3
- Sentences are clear and make sense _____ / 3
- Spelling and punctuation are accurate _____ / 3

Total _____ / 30

Transitions

Adding Information

in addition
additionally
also
moreover
next
further
furthermore
indeed
as well
besides
even more
too
again
not only...but also
and

Contrast

but
however
on the other hand
otherwise
instead
in contrast
yet
nonetheless
on the contrary
though
at the same time
nevertheless

Compare

similarly
likewise
by the same token
in the same way
in similar fashion
in like manner

Giving Examples

for example
for instance
specifically
in particular
to illustrate
to demonstrate

Concession

despite
to be sure
yet
nevertheless
even so
although

Summary

in conclusion
lastly
in sum
in the end
ultimately
finally

Result

therefore
as a result
consequently
as a consequence
for this reason
so
thus

Time Relation or Sequence

first
second
next
in conclusion

Emphasizing

In fact
actually
in other words
namely
indeed

Giving an Alternative

or
either
neither
nor

Your Name   CEA Traditional Essay Map

Instructor Name

Class

Date

                                              Title

        Hook _____

Introduce Essay Topic _____

Body Paragraph 1 Claim _____

Body Paragraph 2 Claim _____

Body Paragraph 3 Claim _____

Thesis _____

        Restate / Rephrase Body Paragraph 1 Claim _____

Supporting Detail for Body Paragraph 1 Claim _____

Evidence from Text _____

Analysis of Evidence _____

Summation _____

        Restate / Rephrase Body Paragraph 2 Claim _____

Supporting Detail for Body Paragraph 2 Claim _____

Evidence from Text _____

Analysis of Evidence _____

Summation _____

        Restate / Rephrase Body Paragraph 3 Claim _____

Supporting Detail for Body Paragraph 3 Claim _____

Evidence from Text _____

Analysis of Evidence _____

Summation _____

        Transition to Concluding Paragraph _____

Restate / Rephrase Thesis _____

Synthesize Body Paragraphs 1, 2, and 3 _____

Concluding Sentence (creatively sum up essay) _____

CEA Traditional Essay Checklist

- ❑ Your Name
- ❑ Instructor Name
- ❑ Class
- ❑ Date

❑ Title

- ❑ Hook — comment ______________________
- ❑ Introduce Essay Topic — comment ______________________
- ❑ Body Paragraph 1 Claim — comment ______________________
- ❑ Body Paragraph 2 Claim — comment ______________________
- ❑ Body Paragraph 3 Claim — comment ______________________
- ❑ Thesis — comment ______________________
- ❑ Restate / Rephrase Body Paragraph 1 Claim — comment ______________________
- ❑ Supporting Detail for Body Paragraph 1 Claim — comment ______________________
- ❑ Evidence from Text — comment ______________________
- ❑ Analysis of Evidence — comment ______________________
- ❑ Summation — comment ______________________
- ❑ Restate / Rephrase Body Paragraph 2 Claim — comment ______________________
- ❑ Supporting Detail for Body Paragraph 2 Claim — comment ______________________
- ❑ Evidence from Text — comment ______________________
- ❑ Analysis of Evidence — comment ______________________
- ❑ Summation — comment ______________________
- ❑ Restate / Rephrase Body Paragraph 3 Claim — comment ______________________
- ❑ Supporting Detail for Body Paragraph 3 Claim — comment ______________________
- ❑ Evidence from Text — comment ______________________
- ❑ Analysis of Evidence — comment ______________________
- ❑ Summation — comment ______________________
- ❑ Transition to Concluding Paragraph — comment ______________________
- ❑ Restate / Rephrase Thesis — comment ______________________
- ❑ Synthesize Body Paragraphs 1, 2, and 3 — comment ______________________
- ❑ Concluding Sentence (creatively sum up essay) — comment ______________________

Your Name CEA Non-Traditional Essay Map

Instructor Name

Class

Date

Title

Thesis _____

Body Paragraph 1 Claim _____

Body Paragraph 2 Claim _____

Body Paragraph 3 Claim _____

Introduction Concluding Sentence / Transition to Body Paragraphs _____

    Restate and Rephrase Body Paragraph 1 Claim _____

Supporting Detail for Body Paragraph 1 Claim _____

Evidence from Text _____

Analysis of Evidence _____

Summation _____

    Restate / Rephrase Body Paragraph 2 Claim _____

Supporting Detail for Body Paragraph 2 Claim _____

Evidence from Text _____

Analysis of Evidence _____

Summation _____

    Restate / Rephrase Body Paragraph 3 Claim _____

Supporting Detail for Body Paragraph 3 Claim _____

Evidence from Text _____

Analysis of Evidence _____

Summation _____

Transition to Concluding Paragraph / Restate and Rephrase the Last Sentence of the Introduction _____

Restate / Rephrase Thesis _____

Synthesize Body Paragraphs 1, 2, and 3 _____

Concluding Sentence (creatively sum up essay) _____

❑ Your Name   *CEA Non-Traditional Essay Checklist*
❑ Instructor Name
❑ Class
❑ Date

❑ Title

❑ Thesis   comment _____

❑ Body Paragraph 1 Claim   comment _____
❑ Body Paragraph 2 Claim   comment _____
❑ Body Paragraph 3 Claim   comment _____
❑ Introduction Concluding Sentence / Transition to Body Paragraphs   comment _____

   ❑ Restate / Rephrase Body Paragraph 1 Claim   comment _____
❑ Supporting Detail for Body Paragraph 1 Claim   comment _____
❑ Evidence from Text   comment _____
❑ Analysis of Evidence   comment _____
❑ Summation   comment _____

   ❑ Restate / Rephrase Body Paragraph 2 Claim   comment _____
❑ Supporting Detail for Body Paragraph 2 Claim   comment _____
❑ Evidence from Text   comment _____
❑ Analysis of Evidence   comment _____
❑ Summation   comment _____

   ❑ Restate / Rephrase Body Paragraph 3 Claim   comment _____
❑ Supporting Detail for Body Paragraph 3 Claim   comment _____
❑ Evidence from Text   comment _____
❑ Analysis of Evidence   comment _____
❑ Summation   comment _____

   ❑ Transition to Concluding Paragraph / Restate and Rephrase the Last Sentence of the Introduction   comment _____
❑ Restate / Rephrase Thesis   comment _____
❑ Synthesize Body Paragraphs 1, 2, and 3   comment _____
❑ Concluding Sentence (creatively sum up essay)   comment _____

Paragraphs and Essays

Example Paragraph and Essay Instructions

On the next pages, three essays serve as examples of *The Baran Method*. The types of essays presented are: argumentative (also called persuasive), explanatory (also informative or expository), and literary analysis. Additionally, there are two paragraphs: one explanatory and one literary analysis.

There are two copies of each piece of writing. The first copy is the original document without notations. The second copy has the claim, evidence, and analysis annotated in corresponding colors and the thesis highlighted in yellow. Transitions are in bold and underlined.

An effective activity is to give writers a copy of the non-annotated essay and have them highlight the claims, evidence, analysis, and thesis and underline or circle transitions. Another highly effective exercise is to have students work in pairs and do the same activity, but with each other's writing.

Remember, there are additional grade-specific paragraph and essay examples at gregbaranwriting.com/resources. The models are organized by grade levels, making it easier to find and work with the material. Feel free to contact me if you have any questions or want personal coaching or group workshops at greg@gregbaranwriting.com or Ph. (760) 459-5597.

Jonathan Student CEA Non-Traditional Essay

Mr. Teacher (Argument)

ELA 9, Per. 4

13 October 2016

Social Media: Beneficial for Teens

Teens should use social media because it positively impacts their lives. First, social networking helps teens build their identities. Secondly, social media helps adolescents learn to communicate and work with others. However, teens should be cautious when using social media since it can negatively affect them by overloading their growing brains with information. Overall, social media does have downsides, but the positives outweigh the negative aspects.

One way social media helps teens is by assisting them find an identity apart from their parents. It is important for teens to find their identities because teens need to understand who they are in relation to the world. Melissa Healy informs us, "Ultimately, it seems, the digital world is simply a new and perhaps more multidimensional place to conduct the age-old work of adolescents - forming identities separate from those of parents" (Teenage). This quote indicates that social media is simply another world where teens build their identities, just as their parents did in the real world when they were teens. Therefore, teens should use social media to help them construct their identity as they enter adulthood.

In addition, teens can learn to communicate and work well with others through social media. Teens can benefit from this because they will learn how to work cooperatively and maturely with co-workers. For example, Megan Mills is a mature teen who uses social media daily to interact with friends, family, and former coaches. This shows a responsible teen who is developing communication skills that are valuable in the social media world and the real world. social skills for when her adult life comes. Consequently, teens should work and spend time online to practice skills that will aid them later.

On the other hand, social media multitasking has its downsides. Multitasking means to do many things on electronic devices at one time. According to Dr. Clifford Nass, "Those kids who are doing it all at the same time are really creating fundamental problems in the way they think" (Sleeping). This quote indicates that teen brains are being overstimulated by multitasking and this may harm their ability to focus on one subject at a time. Therefore, teens should be able to use the internet and social media, but also know the limit or at least limit themselves on their social media usage.

In conclusion, social media clearly has negative aspects, but when used appropriately, the positives outweigh the negatives. Indeed, social media is benefiting teens in many valuable ways. The digital world helps teens create identities apart from their parents, develop communication skills, and learn to work cooperatively with others. However, social media overuse can harm teens unless they learn to limit their usage. Ultimately, social media is a choice, but like the real world, a bit of common sense will help teens achieve a healthy outcome.

Works Cited

Healy, Melissa. "Teenage Social Media Butterflies May Not Be Such a Bad Idea After All." *Los Angeles Times*. 14 October 2010.

Stusser, Michael. "Sleeping With Siri." Twisted Scholar. 2012.

Jonathan Student

Mr. Teacher

ELA 9, Per. 4

13 October 2016

CEA Non-Traditional Essay

(Argument)

Social Media: Beneficial for Teens

==Teens should use social media because it positively impacts their lives (Thesis).== <u>First</u>, social networking helps teens build their identities. <u>Secondly</u>, social media helps adolescents learn to communicate and work with others. <u>However</u>, social media and multitasking can negatively affect teens by overloading their growing brains with information. **<u>Overall</u>**, social media does have downsides, but the positives outweigh the negative aspects.

<u>One way</u> social media helps teens is by assisting them find an identity apart from their parents. It is important for teens to find their identities because teens need to understand who they are in relation to the world. <u>Melissa Healy informs us</u>, "Ultimately, it seems, the digital world is simply a new and perhaps more multidimensional place to conduct the age-old work of adolescents - forming identities separate from those of parents" (Teenage). <u>This quote indicates</u> that social media is simply another world where teens build their identities, just as their parents did in the real world when they were teens. <u>Therefore</u>, teens should use social media to help them construct their identity as they enter adulthood.

<u>In addition</u>, teens can learn to communicate and work well with others through social media. Teens can benefit from this because they will learn how to work cooperatively and maturely with co-workers. <u>For example</u>, Megan Mills is a mature teen who uses social media daily to interact with friends, family, and former coaches. <u>This shows</u> a responsible teen who is developing communication skills that are valuable in the social media world and the real world. social skills for when her adult life comes.

Consequently, teens should work and spend time online to practice skills that will aid them later.

On the other hand, social media multitasking has its downsides. Multitasking means to do many things on electronic devices at one time. **According to** Dr. Clifford Nass, "Those kids who are doing it all at the same time are really creating fundamental problems in the way they think" (Sleeping). **This quote indicates** that teen brains are being overstimulated by multitasking and this may harm their ability to focus on one subject at a time. **Therefore**, teens should be able to use the internet and social media, but also know the limit or at least limit themselves on their social media usage.

In conclusion, social media clearly has negative aspects, but when used appropriately, the positives outweigh the negatives. **Indeed**, social media is benefiting teens in many valuable ways. The digital world helps teens create identities apart from their parents, develop communication skills, and learn to work cooperatively with others. **However**, social media overuse can harm teens unless they learn to limit their usage. **Ultimately**, social media is a choice, but like the real world, a bit of common sense will help teens achieve a healthy outcome.

Works Cited

Healy, Melissa. "Teenage Social Media Butterflies May Not Be Such a Bad Idea After All." *Los Angeles Times*. 14 October 2010.

Stusser, Michael. "Sleeping With Siri." Twisted Scholar. 2012.

Maria Student

Ms. Teacher

ELA 8, Per. 3

24 April 2014

CEA Non-Traditional Essay

(Explanatory)

The Battle of Gettysburg

The Battle of Gettysburg was one of the most important battles of the Civil War. The battle took place between the northern and southern armies near Gettysburg, Pennsylvania. General Lee led the southern armies while General Meade led the northern armies. After the battle, General Meade did not go after the southern army and President Abraham Lincoln was angry about this. Indeed, Lincoln and others felt the Civil War could have ended that day if the northern army had gone after and captured the southern army.

This significant and historic battle occurred on July 1-3, 1863. The battle took place in and around the town of Gettysburg, Pennsylvania. General Lee had invaded the north from the south because he intended to crush the north in this decisive battle, and since many of Lee's soldiers had been injured in previous battles, he felt he had to attack (Battle). This shows Lee's desperation and the fact he knew he had to act. Consequently, Lee needed to beat the northern army at Gettysburg or the south might lose the war altogether.

The leader of the southern army was General Lee and the northern leader was General Meade. Lee had been a commander for many years, but Meade had only been in charge for three days. Both generals led their men in fierce battles that lasted all day long and more men died at Gettysburg than any other battle in the war (Valdez, p. 8). This indicates the tragedy and cost associated with Lee's and Meades decisions. Consequently, over 50,00 soldiers died, but General Lee and General Meade survived the battle, although both died a few years later of natural causes.

When the battle ended, President Abraham Lincoln wanted General Meade to hunt down the southern army. However, General Meade chose not to go after them and many people believe this was a mistake. Lincoln wrote to Meade about Lee, "He was within your easy grasp, and to have closed upon him would, in connection with our other late successes, have ended the war" (Lincoln). This quote shows Lincoln was angry that Meade let Lee slip through his grasp. As a result of Meade's error, the war continued on for two more years.

    In conclusion, the Battle of Gettysburg was a decisive battle in the Civil War. It was important because it was a turning point in the war with the North gaining an advantage. The battle lasted three days and General Meade led the North to victory. However, the sad part of the victory is that if Meade had been more aggressive, the war would have ended and thousands of soldiers' lives would have been saved.

Works Cited

"Battle of Gettysburg." *Britannica Online.* August 2010. web. 10 April 2012. Retrieved from:

    http://www.britannicaonline.com/gettysburgh

Lincoln, Abraham. "Letter from President Lincoln to General George G. Meade." 14 July

    1863. *HistoryPlace.com.* 10 April 2010. Retrieved from:

http://www.historyplace.com/civilwar/lett-6.htm

Valdez, John. *The Civil War.* New York: Pearson, 2010.

Maria Student

Ms. Teacher

ELA 8, Per. 3

24 April 2014

CEA Non-Traditional Essay

(Explanatory)

The Battle of Gettysburg

The Battle of Gettysburg was one of the most important battles of the Civil War (Thesis). The battle took place between the northern and southern armies near Gettysburg, Pennsylvania. General Lee led the southern armies while General Meade led the northern armies. **After the battle**, General Meade did not go after the southern army and President Abraham Lincoln was angry about this. **Indeed**, Lincoln and others felt the Civil War could have ended that day if the northern army had gone after and captured the southern army.

This significant and historic battle occurred on July 1-3, 1863. The battle took place in and around the town of Gettysburg, Pennsylvania. General Lee had invaded the north from the south because he intended to crush the north in this decisive battle, and since many of Lee's soldiers had been injured in previous battles, he felt he had to attack (Battle). **This shows** Lee's desperation and the fact he knew he had to act. **Consequently**, Lee needed to beat the northern army at Gettysburg or the south might lose the war altogether.

The leader of the southern army was General Lee and the northern leader was General Meade. Lee had been a commander for many years, but Meade had only been in charge for three days. Both generals led their men in fierce battles that lasted all day long and more men died at Gettysburg than any other battle in the war (Valdez, p. 8). **This indicates** the tragedy and cost associated with Lee's and Meades decisions. **Consequently**, over 50,00 soldiers died, but General Lee and General Meade survived the battle, although both died a few years later of natural causes.

When the battle ended, President Abraham Lincoln wanted General Meade to hunt down the southern army. **However**, General Meade chose not to go after them and many people believe this was a mistake. **Lincoln wrote to Meade about Lee**, "He was within your easy grasp, and to have closed upon him would, in connection with our other late successes, have ended the war" (Lincoln). **This quote shows** Lincoln was angry that Meade let Lee slip through his grasp. **As a result** of Meade's error, the war continued on for two more years.

  In conclusion, the Battle of Gettysburg was a decisive battle in the Civil War. It was important because it was a turning point in the war with the North gaining an advantage. The battle lasted three days and General Meade led the North to victory. **However**, the sad part of the victory is that if Meade had been more aggressive, the war would have ended and thousands of soldiers' lives would have been saved.

Works Cited

"Battle of Gettysburg." *Britannica Online.* August 2010. web. 10 April 2012. Retrieved from:

http://www.britannicaonline.com/gettysburgh

Lincoln, Abraham. "Letter from President Lincoln to General George G. Meade." 14 July

1863. *HistoryPlace.com.* 10 April 2010. Retrieved from:

http://www.historyplace.com/civilwar/lett-6.htm

Valdez, John. *The Civil War.* New York: Pearson, 2010.

Samantha Student   CEA Traditional Essay

Ms. Teacher   (Literary Analysis)

ELA 12, Per. 4

27 July 2014

Life on Mango Street

Sometimes sad, sometimes painful, and at other times joyous, *The House on Mango Street* by Sandra Cisneros is a gritty and touching story about the life of a young Mexican-American girl named Esperanza. To help us relate to Esperanza's challenging life, Cisneros includes several recurring themes. First, Cisneros shows us the loneliness Esperanza experiences. Next, we see the sadness the young girl endures on the streets of Chicago. However, when Esperanza grows older we get to experience the joys of finding happiness through hard work. In the end, the three themes of loneliness, sadness, and happiness help the reader connect to Esperanza and make this a memorable and meaningful text.

Loneliness and feeling out of place are emotions we have all experienced. Esperanza goes through a lot of both as she struggles to find her place in two worlds. Esperanza states, "In English my name means hope. In Spanish it means too many letters" (10). This passage reveals Esperanza's feelings of loneliness and confusion as she struggles to understand how to fit into two different cultures. As a result, we are able to relate to Esperanza and this theme of loneliness because most of us have experienced similar feelings.

Next, the theme of sadness occurs throughout the book. Cisneros brings the reader close to the pain when Esperanza tells the story of wearing her new dress at a dance. Esperanza says, "Everybody laughing except me, because I'm wearing the new dress, pink and white with stripes and new underclothes and new socks and the old shoes I wear to school, brown and white, the kind I get every September because they last long and they do. My feet scuffed and round, and the heels all crooked that look dumb with this dress, so I just sit" (47). This quote shows the awkwardness and embarrassment Esperanza feels which is brought on by trying to look good and fit in. Consequently, we experience Esperanza's sadness and feel sad for her because we have all felt embarrassed and left out as a kid.

However, the book shows the theme of joy just as intensely as the loneliness and sadness. When Esperanza reaches an age where she can leave home and blossom on her own she shares with the reader her newfound love for writing and the accompanying happiness. Cisneros writes of Esperanza, "I put it down on paper and then the ghost does not ache so much. I write it down and mango says goodbye sometime. She does not hold me with both arms. She sets me free" (110). This quote comes at the end of the book and it shows Esperanza's sense of freedom and accomplishments. Therefore, we see she has survived Mango Street and the streets and she is now thriving and we are happy for her.

In conclusion, Esperanza experienced misfortunes and tragedies. The three themes of loneliness, sadness, and happiness make the book come to life and help us remember how life is challenging and sweet. Like Esperanza, we struggle to find our place in the world, deal with life's struggles, and hopefully eventually experience happiness. In the end, if we can live like Esperanza and see the good at the end of the tunnel we will find happiness after the tragedy.

Works Cited

Cisneros, Sandra. The House on Mango Street. New York: Vintage Contemporaries, 1991.

Samantha Student

Ms. Teacher

ELA 12, Per. 4

27 July 2014

CEA Traditional Essay

(Literary Analysis)

Life on Mango Street

Sometimes sad, sometimes painful, and at other times joyous, *The House on Mango Street* by Sandra Cisneros is a gritty and touching story about the life of a young Mexican-American girl named Esperanza. To help us relate to Esperanza's challenging life, Cisneros includes several recurring themes. **First,** Cisneros shows us the loneliness Esperanza experiences. **Next,** we see the sadness the young girl endures on the streets of Chicago. **However,** when Esperanza grows older we get to experience the joys of finding happiness through hard work. **In the end, the three themes of loneliness, sadness, and happiness help the reader connect to Esperanza and make this a memorable and meaningful text (Thesis).**

Loneliness and feeling out of place are emotions we all have all experienced. Esperanza goes through a lot of both as she struggles to find her place in two worlds. **Esperanza states,** "In English my name means hope. In Spanish it means too many letters" (10). **This passage reveals** Esperanza's feelings of loneliness and confusion as she struggles to understand how to fit into two different cultures. **As a result,** we are able to relate to Esperanza and this theme of loneliness because most of us have experienced similar feelings.

Next, the theme of sadness occurs throughout the book. Cisneros brings the reader close to the pain when Esperanza tells the story of wearing her new dress at a dance. **Esperanza says,** "Everybody laughing except me, because I'm wearing the new dress, pink and white with stripes and new underclothes and new socks and the old shoes I wear to school, brown and white, the kind I get every September because they last long and they do. My feet scuffed and round, and the heels all crooked that look dumb with this dress, so I just sit" (47). **This quote shows** the awkwardness and embarrassment Esperanza feels which is brought on by trying to look good and fit in. **Consequently**, we experience Esperanza's sadness and feel sad for her because we have all felt embarrassed and left out as a kid.

However, the book shows the theme of joy just as intensely as the loneliness and sadness. When Esperanza reaches an age where she can leave home and blossom on her own she shares with the reader her newfound love for writing and the accompanying happiness. **Cisneros writes of Esperanza**, "I put it down on paper and then the ghost does not ache so much. I write it down and mango says goodbye sometime. She does not hold me with both arms. She sets me free" (110). **This quote comes** at the end of the book and it shows Esperanza's sense of freedom and accomplishments. **Therefore**, we see she has survived Mango Street and the streets and she is now thriving and we are happy for her.

In conclusion, Esperanza experienced misfortunes and tragedies. The three themes of loneliness, sadness, and happiness make the book come to life and help us remember how life is challenging and sweet. Like Esperanza, we struggle to find our place in the world, deal with life's struggles, and hopefully eventually experience happiness. **In the end**, if we can live like Esperanza and see the good at the end of the tunnel we will find happiness after the tragedy.

Works Cited

Cisneros, Sandra. <u>The House on Mango Street</u>. New York: Vintage Contemporaries, 1991.

Matthew Student CEA Paragraph
Ms. Teacher (Explanatory)
ELA 10, Period 2
9 May 2016

Kids Serving the Community

The central idea of the text, "Kids Care for Community By Serving Others," focuses on students who give their time to help their community. Some kids are in programs which include being helpers at pet shelters, schools, hospitals, nursing homes, soup kitchens, and city parks. In the article, the author states, "Many children are willing to give time every week to help the less fortunate when they realize the value of helping others." This passage shows that students are willing to give up their time to help their community when they could be hanging out with their friends. In conclusion, students are being helpful and this shows that they care about their community.

Matthew Student CEA Paragraph
Ms. Teacher (Explanatory)
ELA 10, Period 2
9 May 2016

Kids Serving the Community

The central idea of the text, "Kids Care for Community By Serving Others," focuses on students who give their time to help their community. Some kids are in programs which include being helpers at pet shelters, schools, hospitals, nursing homes, soup kitchens, and city parks. **In the article, the author states**, "Many children are willing to give time every week to help the less fortunate when they realize the value of helping others." **This passage shows** that students are willing to give up their time to help their community when they could be hanging out with their friends. **In conclusion**, students are being helpful and this shows that they care about their community.

Olivia Student											CEA Paragraph

Mr. Teacher											(Literary Analysis)

ELA 11, Period 2

13 March 2015

Keats and the Cricket

      John Keats' "On the Grasshopper and the Cricket" uses imagery to portray nature as calm and peaceful. Imagery is language that appeals to the senses. For example, Keats writes, "On a lone winter evening, when the frost / Has wrought a silence, from the stove there shrills / The Cricket's song, in warmth increasing ever." This passage helps us experience and feel the chilly night outside a quiet cabin and then the warmth of the fire inside that attracts a cricket who sings and chirps happily. Therefore, Keats' masterful imagery paints a serene picture that makes us long to be a part of that calm wintery evening.

Olivia Student   CEA Paragraph

Mr. Teacher   (Literary Analysis)

ELA 11, Period 2

13 March 2015

Keats and the Cricket

  John Keats' "On the Grasshopper and the Cricket" uses imagery to portray nature as calm and peaceful. Imagery is language that appeals to the senses. **For example**, Keats writes, "On a lone winter evening, when the frost / Has wrought a silence, from the stove there shrills / The Cricket's song, in warmth increasing ever." **This passage** helps us experience and feel the chilly night outside a quiet cabin and then the warmth of the fire inside that attracts a cricket who sings and chirps happily. **Therefore**, Keats' masterful imagery paints a serene picture that makes us long to be a part of that calm wintery evening.

Made in the USA
Columbia, SC
19 April 2019